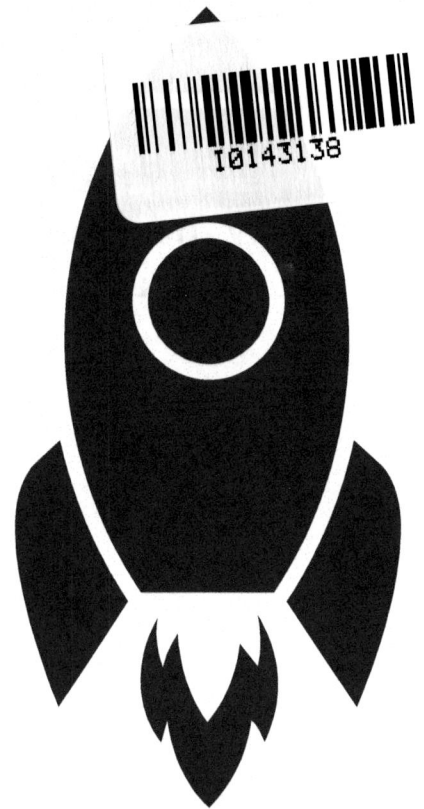

LAUNCH:
THE GREAT SEND-OFF
BY CINDY BRANTON

**This book is dedicated to the graduating class of 2023.
May the Lord be delighted in you as you love people fiercely,
work to uncover and use your gifts, and grow in your
understanding of His transforming truth.
Go and do great things!**

Cindy Branton Writes.
ISBN: 979-8-9878679-0-7

Follow the author @ cindy_branton_writes

Do you want Mrs. Branton to read to your school or church?
Ask your teacher or principal to email her: cindybrantonwrites@gmail.com

"There are far, far better things
ahead than any we leave behind."
— C.S. Lewis

It's happening! It's happening!
It's time to stand and cheer!
This day we've planned and prayed for,
Somehow is finally here!

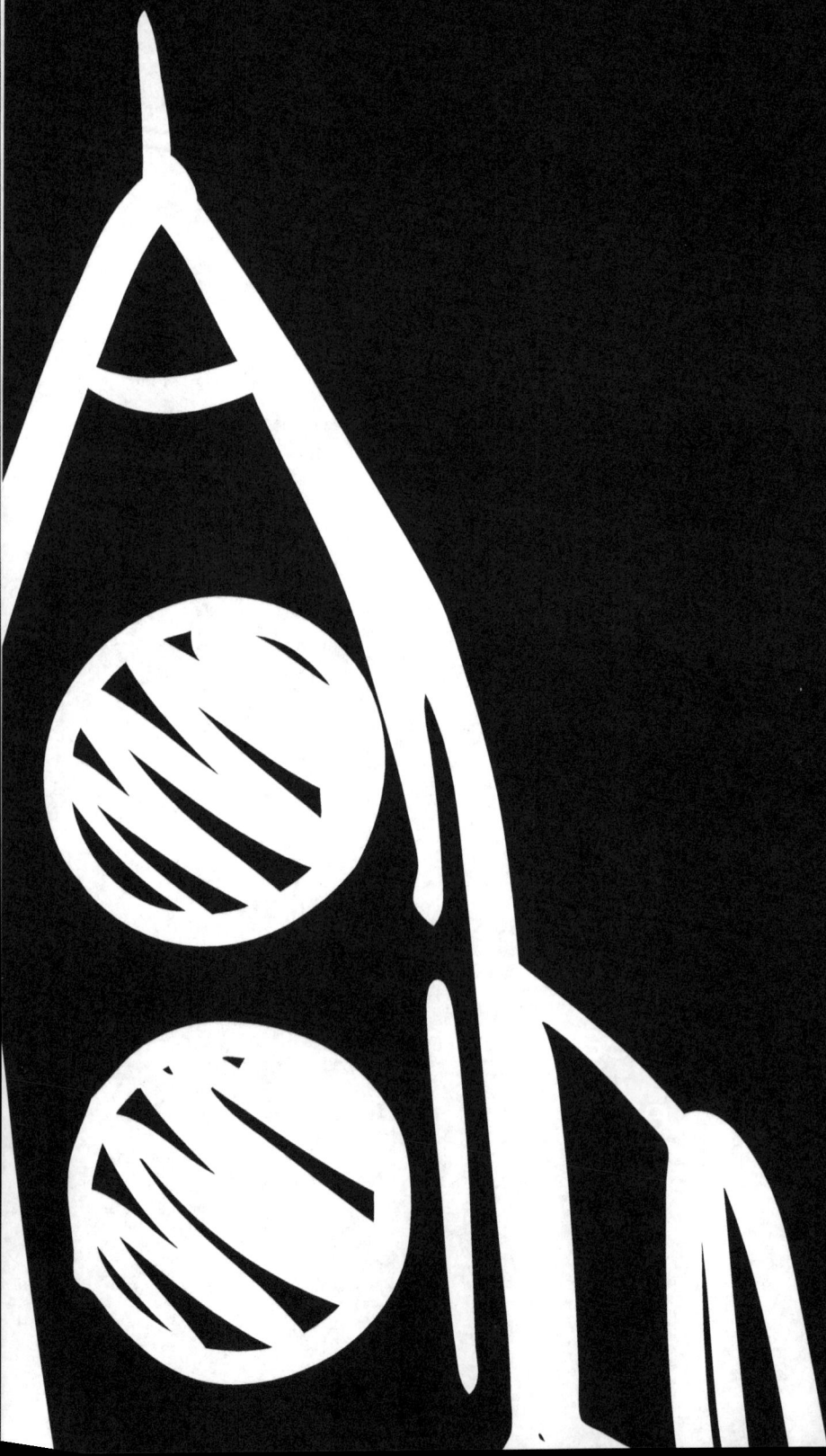

You've worked so hard, you've done your best.
We're all quite proud of you!
Today is set apart
Because today your dreams come true.

We look on you with love,
And we look on you with pride.
We see that God has always
Walked so closely by your side.

Remember when you started,
How the future felt so far?
The finish seemed impossible,
A shiny, distant STAR!

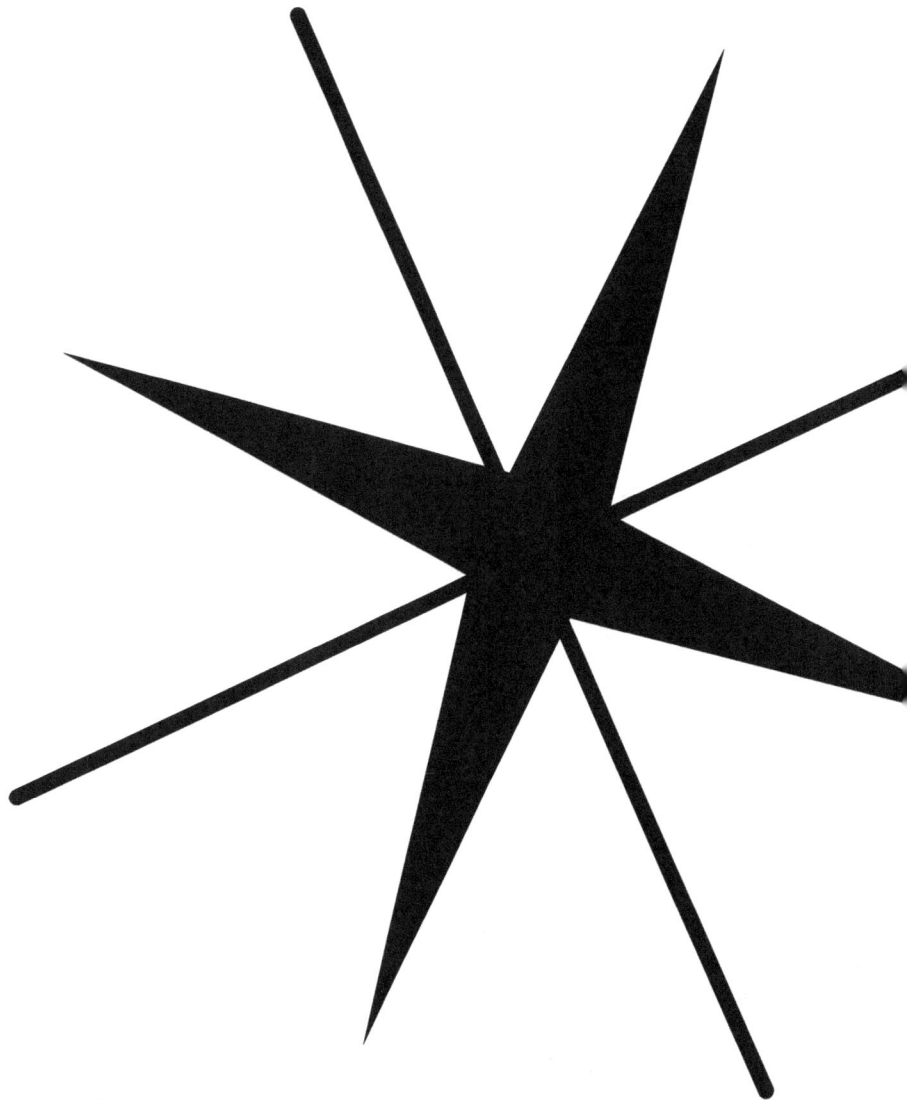

There were days you struggled,
And you wanted to give in.

Even though I walk through the valley of the shadow of death. I will fear no evil.

for you are with me; your rod and your staff, they comfort me. Psalm 23:4

With shiny tears in tiny eyes
You thought you couldn't win.

But every single day,
You've made progress on your goal.
You persevered, not giving up
Determined in your soul.

When troubles felt so monstrous
And tried to swallow you,
You wisely looked to Heaven,
And you asked God what to do.

He looked on you with love,
And He looked on you with pride.
He saw your giant troubles
And He never left your side.

We watched as you pushed forward,
Knowing Jesus was nearby.
You persisted; you kept going
With a tired, stubborn sigh.

When obstacles were great
And your heart was filled with sorrow,
You learned it didn't help to
Borrow troubles from tomorrow.

Deut 31:8 It is the Lord who goes before you. He will be with you; he will not leave you or forsake you. Do not fear or be dismayed."

You overcame your struggles
Learning lessons that you must,
One day at a time,
With the help of those you trust.

Other days held victories
With trophies in your hand!
You won the prize! You earned the praise -
The leader on the stand!

God equipped you with such talent.
We have marveled at your strengths.
It seems that all these gifts will take you
To the greatest lengths!

Could you hear us cheering?
Hear us yelling from the bleachers?
"That one's ours! Belongs to us!"
We are quite excited creatures!

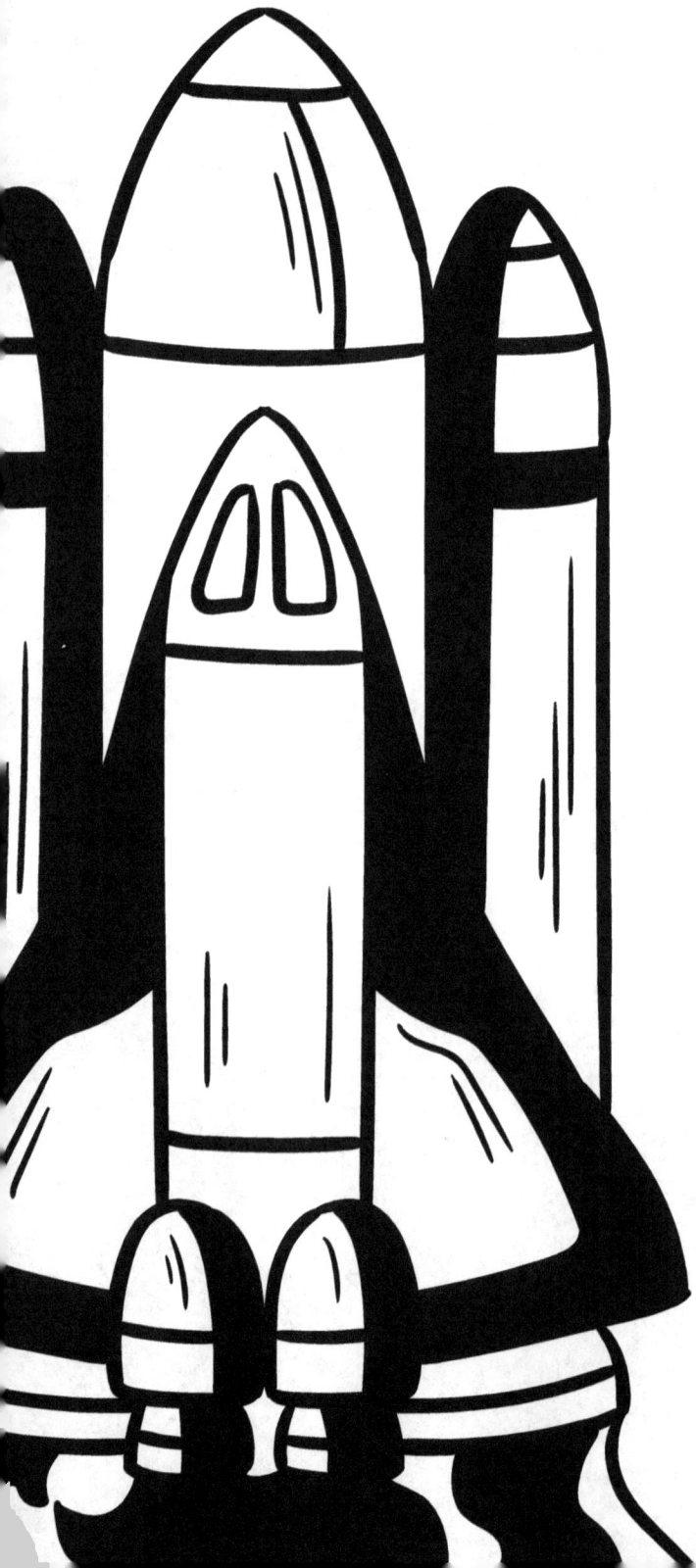

We looked at you with love,
And we cheered you on with pride.
In every single victory,
God was present at your side.

You've learned to build community,
To share the ball and play.
Your teammates then became your friends,
And by your side they stay.

Together in their company,
Sweet memories were created.
We thank God for this gang of love.
In fact, we are elated!

It has been a privilege
to have such an up-close view

Of whom God is designing
In the person that is YOU!

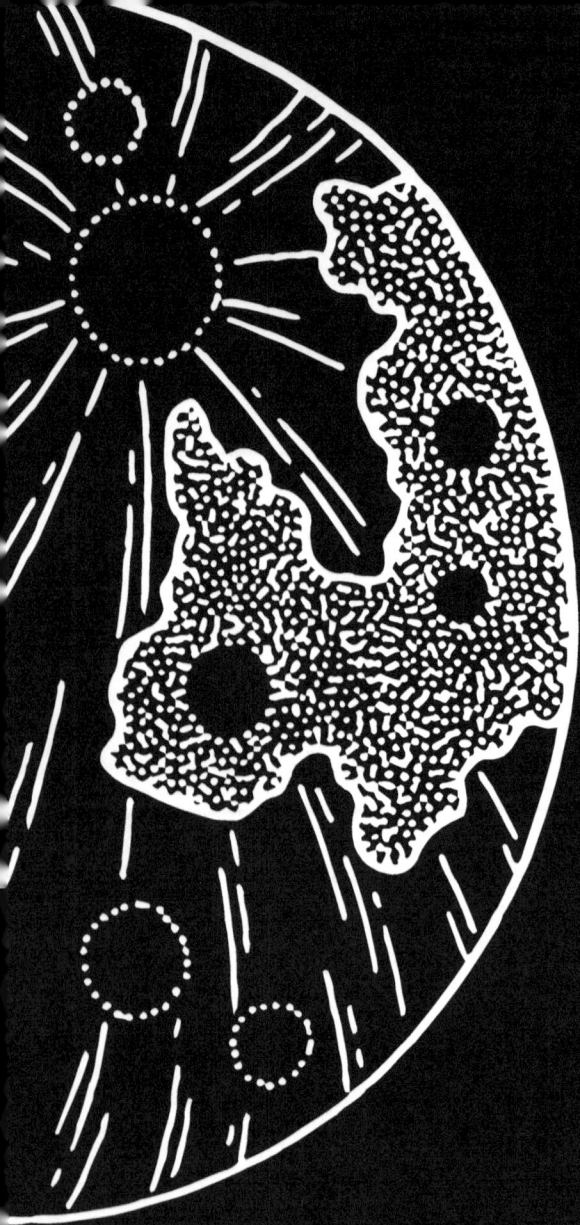

As you launch into your future
And you dive into your dreams,
May the soundtrack to your life
Be our reassuring screams,

"You've got this! You can do it!
You were made for this and more!
You are special! You are loved!
This world is made just to explore!"

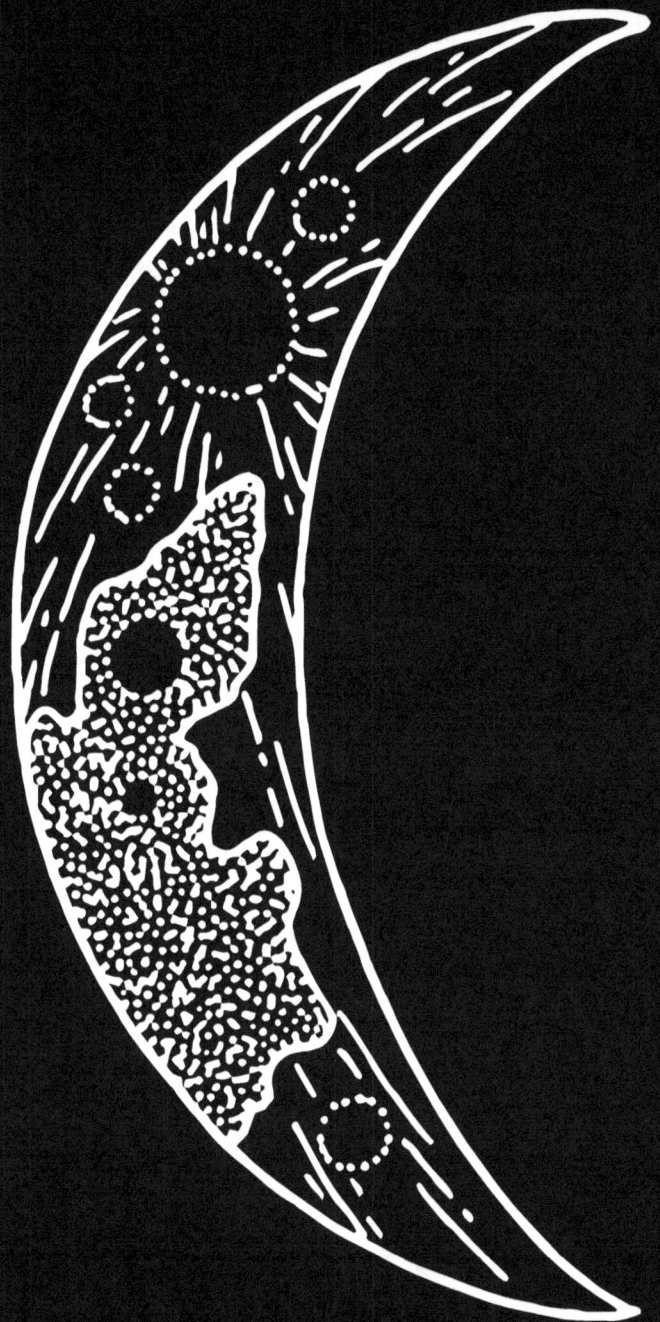

Luke 1:37 For nothing will be impossible with God."

Our God is always with you.
He has promised, so it's true.
His faithful love is constant
In the future and rearview.

What's ahead? Who knows?
Will you build, design, or lead?
Maybe serve the sick
Or set a record for your speed?

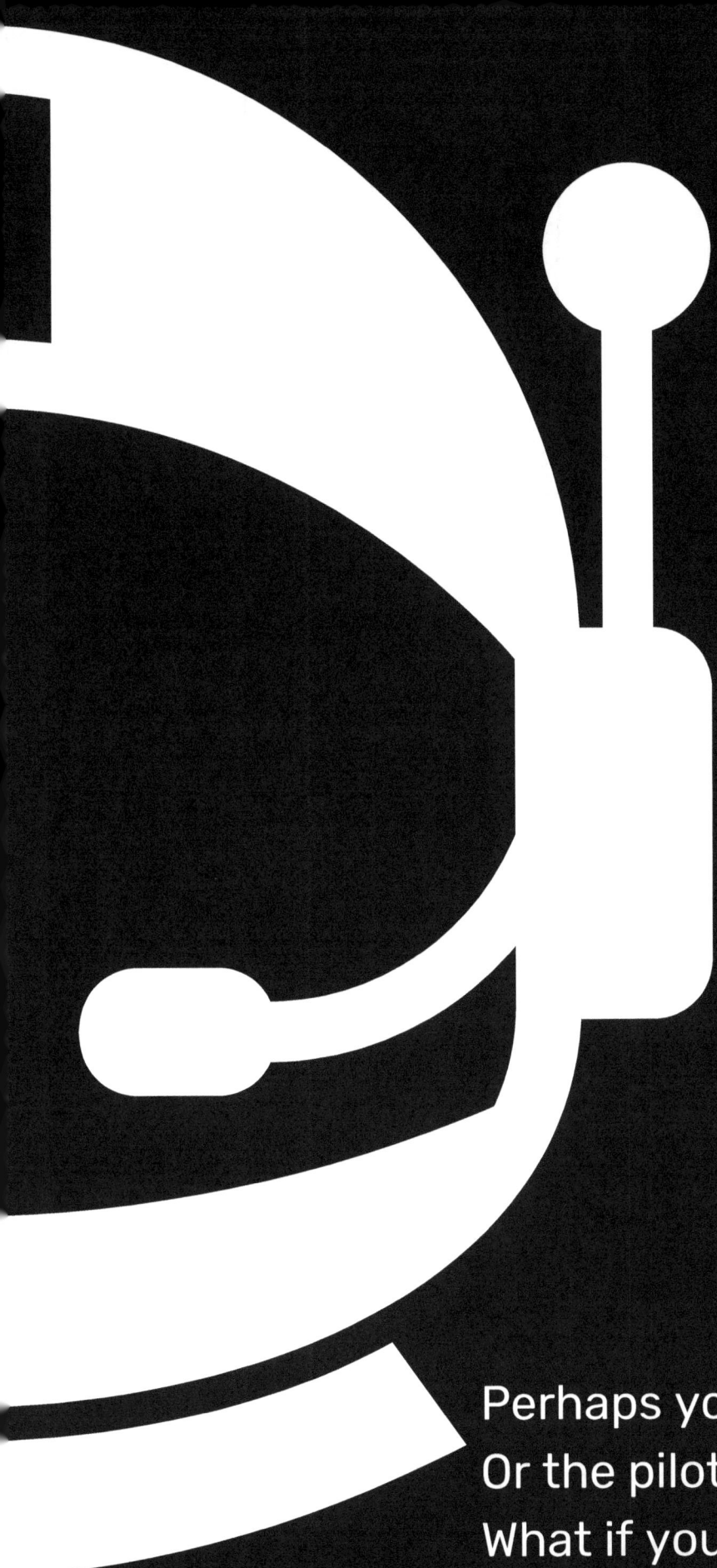

Perhaps you'll be a teacher
Or the pilot of a jet!
What if you're the person
Others thank God that they met?

In all you do, dream big!
May your passions be full-hearted.
Bravely seek adventure!
Hey, you're only getting started!

Today, you're launching out
To an unfamiliar place.
Destiny in front of you,
You've just begun your race!

Take the risks, do the things,
Choose boldness as you go!
Change the world for better,
Share His love, so all will know:

He looks on them with love,
And He treasures them with pride.
This loving God who launched them
Is forever on their side.

Possibilities are endless,
So look forward with a smirk.
The future holds such blessings.
You've got this. It'll work!

3...2...1...
Blast off!!!

NOTES FROM THE LAUNCH TEAM:

Eph 2:10 For we are his workmanship, created in Christ Jesus for good works, which God prepared beforehand, that we should walk in them.

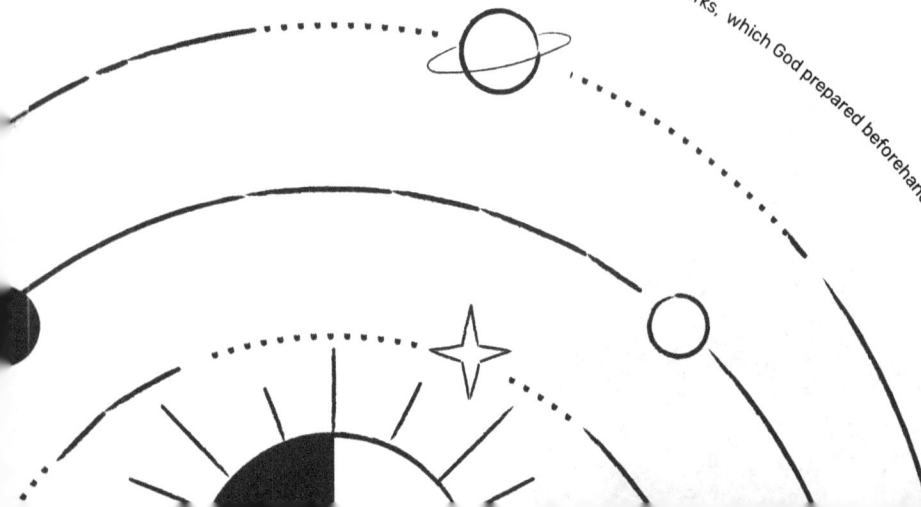

1 Chronicles 16:11 Seek the Lord and his strength; seek his presence continually!